Layers of Life

Stephen Evans

For Joan.

Second Edition: Layers of Life

ISBN: 978-1-953725-16-5

What these strong masters wrote at large in miles, I followed in small copy in my acre; For there's no rood has not a star above it.

Ralph Waldo Emerson

Society and Solitude

Chapters

Foreword

Where are you now? I can only guess.
Surely where the purple-shifted light,
Powered by heart, marks the ancient way
To where the spirit generates each day,
Though here a twinkle only in the night,
In memory, in harmony, to bless.

STEPHEN EVANS

Chapter One

A Gentle Life

The Peaceful Place

I come here often.

About a quarter of a mile down the path behind my home, the trail curves and broadens into an asphalt circle. About 30 feet uphill from a tiny creek that wanders through the northern end of the park, the circle has three occupants: a woodenish bench, a large rock, and me.

I say woodenish because it looks like wood but feels like some sort of composite material, much harder than wood and I suppose more durable. It is painted a wood brown color and is comfortable enough for the occasional visitor like me.

The rock is about three feet by four feet, and maybe 18 inches high of some dark stone, sedimentary I think because it is formed in thin layers, shale perhaps, though flecks here and there glitter like diamonds. Maryland is home to a black shale deposit known as the Marcellus shale, which grew up about 400 million years ago when the state was a shallow sea. The rock has secrets, I can tell, maybe fossils hidden inside, but it is not telling, not me anyway.

It occurs to me that both rock and bench will be here long after me. They were here first, and so that seems fair.

The bench faces east and the sun warms my right check, while the breeze cools my left hand. There is little noise from cars, and only the occasional plane overhead. Surprising for a densely populated area, the ambient noise is mostly natural. I close my eyes to listen.

There's a wood dove behind me, a mockingbird up and to the right, a smaller sweet-voiced bird I can't identify somewhere in front. In the distance the brazen call of the crows disrupts the serenity from time to time. The trees in their buds rustle quietly now – their voices will grow with their leaves. The loudest sound is the crackle of squirrels as they chase though the dried leaves, until the hammering of a sapsucker opens my eyes

I turn to locate him. The red headdress makes it easy. A tall slender tree has fallen across the creek, only to be caught partly upright by another tree on the opposite bank. The sapsucker is traversing the fallen tree looking for soft spots. The business of life goes on.

I always think of my father here. We used to stop here on our walks in his last year; a great walker most of his life, it was as far as he could go, or maybe as far as I thought he could. But he didn't mind stopping. I think it was peaceful for him too.

I have had other peaceful places.

This is the closest.

The others are far away in space or time or both.

Lake of the Isles was just down the block from our house in Minneapolis, and I absorbed its peace daily during the dissolution of my marriage. It was also gracious enough to inspire a story I have been writing for twenty years now.

Some of the peaceful others I have only visited once. Mallory Dock in Key West – though you wouldn't think to find peace in the middle of that circus atmosphere. It also inspired a story.

A pond in Pipestone Minnesota where wings of dragonflies conducted a symphony I could not hear.

A spot outside Devil's Tower, the quietest place I have ever been, where the deer and the antelope play.

Another south of Yellowstone where the white noise of waterfall enveloped me in solitude.

All these I have celebrated in books, and hope to celebrate in person once more in this life.

I can't remember any I had as a child. Perhaps it was just my bedroom, where I hid in my books. I was an inside child, asthma probably as formative in my growth as any factor. There was a tree in our backyard with a swing. Maybe that was one: I wrote a poem about it years later.

I hadn't realized before this how many of my peaceful places I have written about. They are important to me no doubt. I have a brain that is at best restless and at worst relentless. Imagining these places helps to calm me, to keep in check the unbounded notions I am prone to even now.

I hope everyone has a peaceful place, or more than one. We need them in this anxious world.

But if you don't, feel free to borrow one of mine.

I'll be the one smiling when you get there.

No One Expects Metasequoia Glyptostroboides

I like trees.

I'm not exactly sure when this relationship began. But I think it might have been in 1970, on a family vacation to California. We flew out to San Francisco and drove down the coast to LA, stopping for a few days in Yosemite, where I took 1000 or so bad photos, which are now bad and unwatched slides. And somewhere around there we also saw Redwoods.

There were many of them, I think, but not a whole forest of them. And I'm not sure but I believe we saw one that you could drive through. I don't really remember how they looked, exactly, or what I thought. But I remember how they made me feel. I remember being surrounded by a sense of immense age, impressed with the realization that there were beings on this earth measured in frames outside the human.

That was nearly fifty years ago, a long time for me, a moment for them. For some reason over the last few years, I have felt a strong desire to see them again. I'm not sure why, or why now. Maybe I hope something so ancient will make me feel young again. Or maybe just a worry that they, along with so much else, may soon disappear, from erosion or drought or acid rain or who knows. Things disappear – I have learned that. But they also appear.

There is a path behind my house where I walk once or twice most weeks, for the last decade or so. The crooked tree is there, so is the straight one, and most of the others I have written about. I was walking a few days ago when I saw this one.

It's a redwood. Not a California Redwood, but a Dawn redwood, Metasequoia glyptostroboides, an Asian cousin. It won't grow as tall as Sequoia sempervirens or a large around as Sequoiadendron giganteum. But it is a redwood. A beautiful one. And it had been there, a hundred yards from my home, for years.

So keep an eye out for redwoods. My new motto is: No one expects Metasequoia glyptostroboides.

Hope

Behind my home there is a young tree, a sapling I suppose, planted a few years ago to replace another that had died. It's a maple I think and this year was the first that the leaves turned that rich autumn red.

Most of them are gone now, fallen as is usual, but at the very top of the tree there is a cluster that hangs on. For some reason, every time I see them, they give me hope. I think we may have to rephrase Emily Dickinson a bit:

Hope is the tree with red leaves
That linger at the top
And waver in the winter wind
And never wish to drop

The Big Reveal

The leaves are fading fast now, falling in waves and beginning to shower the ground in brown.

The colors are dim this year, I suppose because the rain was limited. The connection between water and color is a mysterious one, an algorithm I cannot fathom, except to say that just enough, at just the right time, is a condition of brilliance.

But one thing I do appreciate about the leafless trees is the revelation of structure. I have long been fascinated_by this, drawn to something elemental in the vision. I wonder why each tree happened to grow in that unique and complex way - what combination of water, wind, heredity and happenstance has led to this specific existential architecture.

My favorites are the trees at night, dark grey trunks and branches barely revealed against the deeper sky. On a clear night, the stars shine between the branches, as though the leaves have been reincarnated as celestial bodies.

Maybe that's what winter is for, to drop the veneer and let the heaven show through.

The Language of Trees

The trees were winking at me this morning.

Or maybe it was morse code.

Tiny brights lights kept going on and off, as if someone was hitting a switch.

But irregular, like a cipher.

I finally figured it out.

It was the light of the sun refracting through raindrops as the leaves moved in the breeze.

Nature speaks to us.

I hope we are listening.

The Architecture of Trees

The architecture of trees fascinates me. How do the branches know how to grow?

Complexity theory?

Fibonacci Sequences?

Artificial intelligence?

A complex algorithm it must be.

In searching for its own light, the branch serves the tree. What does the branch know of the tree?

The result seems always the same: Spare beauty against the blue.

Tree Song

I don't know why the caged bird sings. But I think I may have finally figured out why the others do.

I take walks every day down a wooded path behind my home. Sometimes so many birds are singing it sounds like a choir. Other times there are only one or two at each turn of the path. Occasionally the songs sound like a dialogue, sometimes a Bach canon. But most often the sounds are clearly ecstatic, a brimming forth of some secret joy.

I believe I have discovered the source of that joy. Each bird is singing about how beautiful its tree is. How delicately shaped each leaf as it twists in the breeze. How the broad canvas of the whole creates ever evolving shadows on the ground. How the Fibonacci architecture of the branches leads right up to the sky.

Birds never sing about what time they have to get to the bird feeder, or whether they need a bath, or the bird next door, or even that tree they saw two weeks ago. They only sing of the beauty in front of them.

Each bird sings in its own language. Birds are very smart; each knows all the languages of all the birds. But when they sing of trees they sing in their own tongue, the one they hold in their heart.

And when they fly to the next tree, birds sing about how beautiful that tree is. And I agree with them.

I have never seen a tree that was not beautiful, from smallest sapling to startling senior. And unique – no tree the same as any other– even the aspen trees (which reproduce by what is called root sprouting and are in a sense one tree) are genetically identical but never quite the same in appearance. I wonder sometimes if the beauty of trees has something to do with their uniqueness—and if we were more aware of it in humankind, we might see more beauty in each other.

Do the trees listen to the birds? I think so. Do they appreciate the praise? I'm not so sure. The lives of trees seem unconcerned with birds, or squirrels, or humans. They have their own purposes in their long lives.

What beauty do trees sing about?

I doubt we will ever know.

The Leaf or the Shadow

I was taking a walk at noon or so, when a leaf fell from a tree a few feet in front of me. Even on the asphalt path, I could see the darker shadow of the descending leaf, and I watched them both. The leaf as it fell twisted and turned, and lurched this way and that in the breeze, almost as though it were trying to escape the shadow below it. With each twist and lurch, the shape of the shadow altered, even though the leaf itself did not change shape. When it finally reached the ground and joined the waiting shadow, the shape of the leaf and shape of the shadow matched perfectly under the sun.

One of these is like life, I thought.

But is it the leaf?

Or the shadow?

So May We All

I wrote this last year:

"Well, I made it to 65. I am grateful for the experiences along the way, especially the ones that ended up as stories, or may yet. So grateful also to the family and friends here and gone who made it such a rich unforgettable (I hope) journey.

When I started typing this, 65 came out as ^%; as I had the caps lock on. That may be a sign of the coming times, and yet appropriate; I plan to live life like the cap lock is on from now on. SO MAY WE ALL."

Most of us had no idea what 2020 had in store for the world, the human world anyway. My life, or the living of it, didn't work out as I planned, the CAP LOCK lock did not go on as I had enisioned it. But then that is true of most of my life, and maybe most of life.

There is a tree across the way from me. It has a double trunk, split in two almost at the ground. One tree or two, I don't know. An oak or something else solid and strong.

The right trunk is maybe forty feet tall, and leaves are just starting to bud. The other goes up thirty feet or so, where the trunk is twisted, and tapers almost to a point. A tornado maybe came close and wrenched off the top. But I had not noticed until today that out of that ragged ending, slender branches reached a good ways, buds perched on the ends, just as with its twin.

It reminded me of a time I was driving through Yellowstone, a year to two after fires had ravaged a third of the park. Beneath the blackened remnants of the pines, saplings beyond count had thrust up through the charcoal earth. Most were only inches high. But the forest was healing itself. I wrote this:

Seek the path
Of vital devastation.
In the white pines,
Spring forward.

So may we all, cap locks or no.

Perfect Fit

I bought a new toaster oven recently when my old one stopped turning off by itself. The new one looked similar to the old one, but the rack for the toast was terrible, incredibly difficult to get in or out, rattling the entire toaster every time I opened the door.

Who could design such a flawed device I thought? Where is the quality control? Where is the pride?

Then one day after several weeks of struggling to save my english muffins, I took the rack out, turned it upside down, and put it back in.

Of course it worked. Smooth. Effortless. A perfect fit. I have no idea why. It looks absolutely the same to me either way.

Maybe that's why my life seems to turn upside down pretty often all on its own.

It is still seeking that perfect fit.

Flipping the Omelet

Very few people who have eaten my cooking realize that I am an expert cook.

My topic today is flipping the omelet:

Never flip an omelet from the center. Always flip from the side. If you are right-handed, flip from the left side. If you are left-handed, flip from the right.

Never flip from out to in. Flip in to out if you must.

Never flip from back to front or front to back. It just confuses the omelet. Not to mention the cook.

These instructions apply to many areas of life, especially if butter is involved.

The Blue Cap

She wears a dark blue raincoat on this cloudy day, and a lighter blue cap, something out of the sixties. I can imagine her then, a young woman, wearing one to a party, dazzling with her golden hair and brilliant smile, charming them all.

Now her hair is white. And white tennis shoes. Always the white shoes.

And alone. Always alone. Except for the dog.

Her dog is smallish and also white, like most of the dogs in this community. For some reason, they are the canine of choice, maybe because they don't eat much or fit just so on an eighty-year old lap.

As she walks, she sways side to side. Maybe her hips don't work as they used to or she is shielding her knees. Still she walks. Twice a day. Every day. At a good pace relatively.

Holding tight to the leash. As though something about it keeps her upright.

I walk past her and smile, saying Good Afternoon. She doesn't seem to recognize me, though we have passed a few times before. Her face brightens and she smiles, but she doesn't speak back. Unused now to speaking to anyone, except her children on the phone every few weeks.

She is alone. Always alone. Except for the dog, who is now the beneficiary of all the love and care she has stored up since her husband passed.

So she walks every day. Rain or shine. In peril of falling every step it seems to me. I worry for her.

She is alone. Yet there are many like her here in this community. She passes them every day. They have never spoken yet they know each other.

As she passes me, I turn and watch for a second.

Maybe this is not her story. Maybe she has a family close to her, who visit most days, like my next door neighbor. Maybe her husband does the laundry and she walks the dog for exercise. I don't really know.

But as I imagine her, she is a reminder.

And a warning.

And an inspiration.

I will find my blue cap.

Beautiful Things

Recently, I subscribed to an internet program that is supposed to help with relaxation and meditation, using images of nature accompanied by peaceful music. Lots of flutes. I like to listen while I work; it cuts the silences of working from home.

I was reading one day, listening, glancing up occasionally to see what beautiful thing was on. Suddenly I felt sad, but I wasn't sure why. After a while, I realized that I was sad because I would never actually see the beautiful things that were on the screen. Except on a screen. I may never visit a beach in Thailand at sunset, or the Alps at sunrise. Because of time. Because of distance. Because of money. Because of age or health. It is world of beautiful things but our time here is short and for most of us our resources are limited.

And then I thought, yet here I am now seeing these things on television at least. That is seeing of a kind. Some of them I might have guessed at their existence. But many I would likely never have known about, except for this seeing. And if the images in this program are beautiful, there are many more beautiful images, stunning and extraordinary and strange, shown on TV and the Internet these days, on channels dedicated to them.

And not just natural beauty. Art is more accessible than ever before. Major museums are putting images of masterpieces within the reach of everyone at a click or two. And music also. Sites stream Bach and Mozart, Schubert and Prokofiev (my personal favorite), and so many more, many I have never heard of. Fifty years ago– no make that one hundred years ago, I forget how old I am–you would have had to attend a concert in Oslo or Vienna or New York to hear them.

This is a miraculous age of beautiful things, offered to us wherever we turn. I'm sure that they are more beautiful to experience in person. I would rather see them from a concert in Oslo, an evening at the Met in New York, or flying over the Alps at sunrise (okay, I might have to close my eyes at that one).

But even in seeing them in this removed way, they are still beautiful. And I can see more of them this way than I could possibly see in a lifetime. That's a gift, and something to be grateful for.

Classic

Some months ago I took a job with a fairly long commute, about an hour each way. In the morning on the way in to work, I listen to the news (and the traffic reports). In the evening, I turn on WETA– 90.9 FM - the publicly supported classical music station in Washington DC.

I have enjoyed classical music since high school, when my amazing choir teacher Henry Benedict introduced us to English madrigals, Bach motets, and Palestrina Masses (I wonder how often current students have this opportunity). From there I went on to studying voice and giving the occasional classical recital between more frequent ventures into musical theater. But until my job change, most of my recent forays into classical music were occasional late night explorations of YouTube (a musical treasure trove).

It's a little different listening to classical music on the radio. The programming consists of drive-time selections (though I have not figured out the selection process), nothing too long, or too bizarre, well-known classical pieces from the 18th and 19th century, heavy one the B's (Bach, Brahms, Beethoven), interspersed with some well-chosen earlier and later works from Byrd to Bernstein. And though I am pretty familiar with some of the works, hearing them one after another, day after day, has been enlightening.

I have been struck by a few recent realizations. I am amazed at the extraordinary number of talented musicians from all parts of the world, the brilliant composers I have never heard of, the seemingly inexhaustible variety of composition and tonality.

But over and above the things, I am conscious of how lucky we are to have these works available everyday everywhere. Three hundred years ago these experiences were reserved for kings and princes (except those you could hear in church). Two hundred years ago, it was usually the wealthy who could afford such performances. One hundred years ago, recordings were few and far between.

But now – who could count the number and variety of performances available in the air and online? Well, maybe Google – there are as I write 220,000,000 hits for the words musical performance.

When the aliens come back and attempt to determine our greatest achievement as a species, I think music, specifically classical music, may be at the top of the human hit parade.

The Seventh

The Third is heroic.

The Fifth is iconic.

The Ninth is a miracle.

But of all of Beethoven's Nine symphonies, my favorite has always been the Seventh.

I don't know why exactly. It just appealed to me immediately, the rhythms and melodies, the energy pulsing through yet not overwhelming. More subtle than the others, yet somehow truer to itself.

And there is a joy that runs through it, different from the Ode to Joy of the Ninth, more self-contained and pure, especially in the Allegretto, the second movement. You can hear something similar sometimes in Bach and Mozart. I don't know what it is. But I think of it as the joy of a master engaged only in the work.

Just vague impressions I know.

Hard to explain.

How do you judge a symphony? Or greatness? Or art?

Mozart and Shakespeare are at the top for me. Old Bach is not far behind. Michelangelo perhaps belongs near. And somewhere not too far down the list is Beethoven.

To some extent, maybe a great extent, it is a personal decision. You could break it down into categories I suppose. Originality. Breadth of expression. Depth of emotion. Uniqueness. Capacity.

But in saying that the Seventh is my favorite, I am not really judging it. I'm just expressing a preference. Though somewhere down deep maybe there is little difference, since judgement has to be based on something, and if you go far enough down there are likely personal choices supporting whatever criteria you elect.

So I was delighted today, listening to it on the radio, when the announcer noted that the Seventh was Beethoven's favorite too. When asked why it was not as well-known as the others, Beethoven reportedly said: Because it's better.

Who am I to argue with the master?

The Miracle in the Background

I was in Starbucks today with my usual vanilla latte, sitting by the front window and checking email on my phone. There was some music playing, Starbucks music, coffeehouse music, four or five instruments, somewhat eclectic, part-classical, part Braveheart. And it occurred to me that in the easy availability we have lost sight of the miracle of music, the richness and complexity and joy of it. Or I have anyway, much of the time. How different it must have been to have to wait for Beethoven to hear Beethoven. It is hard for me to imagine a world where I couldn't put Beethoven on the stereo or ipod (or phone). I wouldn't want to give up this availability. But I have resolved to try and really listen more often. And I wonder - what other miracles are there in background, waiting for attention?

We Shall Go On to the End

On this D-Day anniversary, I have to admit I don't watch war movies, even very good films like *The Battle of the Bulge* or *Saving Private Ryan*. I don't watch anything violent if I can help it, as I don't want to invite that into my psyche; these images are far more powerful than we understand.

But recently, by some coincidence, I happen to have been reading war books. First, *The Guns of August* by Barbara Tuchman, about the start of World War II, and the epic mistakes and misapprehensions that led to that tragic conflict. And *The Enormous Room* by E. E. Cummings, a brilliant depiction of a French prison camp during that war.

And last night, I happened on a recording of Winston Churchill's stirring speech to the House of Commons following the Word War II battle of Dunkirk, and remembered then the slim thread upon which civilization may hang.

"We shall go on to the end, we shall fight in France, we shall fight on the seas and oceans, we shall fight with growing confidence and growing strength in the air, we shall defend our Island, whatever the cost may be, we shall fight on the beaches, we shall fight on the landing grounds, we shall fight in the fields and in the streets, we shall fight in the hills; we shall never surrender, and even if, which I do not for a moment believe, this Island or a large part of it were subjugated and starving, then our Empire beyond the seas, armed and guarded by the British Fleet, would carry on the struggle, until, in God's good time, the New World, with all its power and might, steps forth to the rescue and the liberation of the old."

Most in the US Armed Services who have died in action did not do so to preserve our country, or our rights. The US as a nation has not been directly threatened since the war of 1812. But thousands of US servicemen died (in Europe and the Pacific, in Korea and Vietnam, in Afghanistan and Bosnia and Somalia and Iraq and Syria) attempting to save civilization, and more, trying to create a better world. We honor their service and sacrifice most by continuing to do so.

What We Can Do

There is no answer I suppose - an open society will always be at risk. But it is cruel and senseless. And there are tens of thousands more who die each day who don't make the news, each as important. It can be overwhelming. And deeply confusing. Life goes on. More will die tomorrow.

We do what we can to bring something beautiful into the world.

Will it balance?

Probably not.

But it is what we can do.

What If

I became a vegetarian not because it was more healthy or even more ethical, but because I did not want to add to the anguish in the world. I have never regretted that decision, or even seriously questioned it.

But what if every one was a vegetarian? What if overnight some switch was thrown and no one ate eat meat any longer?

Sounds great, doesn't it? But I wonder what would happen to the billions of animals raised for food around the globe? Would they starve? Would we have massive euthanasia because we couldn't afford to feed them?

And suppose it was a gradual transition, no massive change, just fewer and fewer animals slaughtered. That would certainly mean fewer and fewer animals raised. Is it really better for them never to live than to live a while?

Take away the quality of life issues: if the life was comfortable and the death painless, which would be better—some life, or none? If you had to make that same choice for yourself, or your family, which would you choose?

Animals cannot choose the life we give them. But they can't choose the life we don't give them either.

Peace

I was sitting outside on my porch today reading for a few hours. All during that time birds came visiting. First there was a beautiful jay, stunning blue and quiet for once, nestled into a spot in the sun just a few feet away. Then a robin. Then a few grosbeaks. Some sparrows. Dad's favorite wren who lives in the azalea next door. A woodpecker on the nearby tree. Others I couldn't name. And now there is a doe settled in the shadowed grass about 100 feet away, testing the breeze, with a young buck standing close. Just living. All just living.

Was that so hard, Life?

Layers of Life

Just outside my patio there is a large azalea bush. It blooms beautiful pink-orange blossoms for about two weeks each year, usually in May. The rest of the year it looks like most any large green bush.

I was sitting by the sliding glass doors that lead to the patio today and I noticed that there was a small swarm of gnats circling in chaotic patterns over the top of the bush. I had never noticed them before. Then I began to think of all the life associated with that one azalea bush.

There are the gnats, who seemed to find it for the moment entirely fascinating, and also a family of sparrows who make it their year-round home, along with a pair of wrens, and family (the baby who keeps trying to get into the apartment and makes me wonder if it is my Dad reincarnated because he loved wrens and loved to sing) and the cardinal pair who drop by for periodic visits along with the butterflies who arrive happily during that colorful two weeks, and disappointedly the rest of the year and the curious bees, especially the large bumblebees who find it intriguing along with the juncos, winter residents, and the wood doves, who love to sun themselves at the base of it next to the ants who make their homes in the soil and climb the wall beside it to get the larger view while beneath the soil, mixed in with the roots, who knows what denizens lurk—grubs and worms and for 16 and a half years, surely cicadas too, to say nothing of a teeming microbiome wholly unknown to me as I stare out.

Sorry—I've been reading Kerouac again.

Life is more than we know.

Attention is a path to joy.

The Bug and the Blade

I was looking out my back window this Sunday morning and about ten feet away I noticed a bug climbing a blade of grass. I shouldn't have been able to see something so small at that distance, but the blade was angled just so that the bug glinted like polished bronze in the sun. She struggled up that smooth green slippery surface until it bent down and was hidden.

And it struck me then how vast the world is, and how very very tiny is our part in it. And how many many stories come and go without notice. And how writers, the ones who notice and record, have an impossible and important job to do.

I waited to see if it would fling her into the air when she reached the end, but neither bug nor blade reappeared. Like Frosts' birches, it set her set her gently down again onto the earth, bent for the moment by her passing.

I kept watch a good while. One could do worse than be a writer of notices.

Time to Sing

So there's this cricket.

He comes to visit every August, and he stays in the wall of my bedroom. His living room seems to be the window frame by my bed, I think because it is the best place to sing. It is long and slender, almost like an echo chamber.

He does like to sing.

Especially at night.

My hearing is pretty sensitive. And I find I am unable to fall asleep while he (or she – we've never actually met in person) is serenading me.

So if I have been a little grump lately I apologize. I am not getting as much sleep as usual.

Not to be un-neighborly, but I have tried to convince him to move. I drop essential oils in a small hole in the window frame, which are supposedly too aromatic for the species. I shoot compressed air down the chamber, hoping to convince him a hurricane is approaching and he should take (other) shelter. I put in an ultrasonic device.

None of these have worked. But I refuse to take more drastic measures. I don't want to hurt him; I just want him to find another place to sing.

I have also tried ways to co-exist. Noise generators. Ear plugs. These help, but not enough.

I thought perhaps he might be insulted at the lengths I would go to avoid his song. If someone did that while I was singing, I think I would get the hint. But he keeps on singing, even knowing that he is singing to himself.

But it occurred to me this morning that we are the same in this way. He keeps on singing whether anyone is listening. I keep on writing whether anyone is reading.

I'm luckier than he. Once his song is done, it is gone. My words will last a bit. I can't say how long. But longer than I will, likely. And that is one of the things that keeps me writing.

He is singing now as I write this. And as I am singing in my own way here, I think: "keep singing little one".

Everyone needs their time to sing.

Days of the Cicadas

There was a 1962 movie called Day of the Triffids, starring of all people Howard Keel, about an alien invasion. That is what it feels like around my home today. Brood X has arrived.

Brood X is the term for this brood of cicadas, which has lived underground for 17 years, to emerge for a short time to mate and lay eggs. There are billions of them all over the Mid and North Atlantic seaboard in the US. And my home seems to be Ground Zero.

A cicada, if you have never seen one, is (in this recent incarnation), a winged insect maybe an inch and a bit long. They are surprisingly gentle flyers, and most prefer to perch on the trunks of trees. Oak and beech so far seem to be the favorites as far as I have seen. The din that they make is loud and exotic, even otherworldly, as if stepping outside you have stepped through to a jungle, or another planet. These are the Days of the Cicadas.

I have been around long enough to have seen them before. I have memories of a high school baseball game, the tall wooden poles of the field lighting almost invisible under the covering horde. There are other broods, but this one is the largest by far.

Unlike other swarms, the cicadas do no harm, but harm comes to them. They are something of a feast for the local bird population. I have heard that they are edible by humans, but I have seldom been more thankful to be a vegetarian.

After they have mated, they descend to the ground, and wait patiently to die. This is what fascinates me about them. Seventeen years in the ground for a few moments in the light. I have yet to unpack the richness of this metaphor.

But something about them I find heroic. Maybe it is that at the end of their lives they find the energy to create. I root for them as

I see them flying into the trees, rooting for myself in the process.

The Butterfly and the Bee

As we all know, I have a low threshold of fascination. Today for example as I have been working on a book, I have also been keeping an eye on my petunias. I have never had petunias before, so perhaps that accounts for some of the fascination. But really what garnered my attention for the last few hours is two visitors: a butterfly and an bee.

Initially actually I was watching a pail of water. It's very hot today and I had set out what I hoped would be a makeshift birdbath. As I watched the pail, the water looked still and undisturbed. But the bright sun threw a reflection of the water onto the roof of my porch. In the reflection I could see the water moving, from the wind or maybe convection currents as the water heated in the brutal daylight. The reflection also showed the rippling waves as my gift evaporated. I felt like I had my own little Plato's cave, except the reflection was truer than the actual. Though I suspect that was true of Plato's as well.

But then the butterfly appeared, a large one, likely a swallowtail (my older brother would know), black wings with blue and gold spots. She (I think) kept flying around the weeds in my little garden. I have weeds in my garden, a lot of them this year. I leave them there because I don't hurt anything if I don't have to and they seem to feel the same. Anyway, the butterfly kept landing on one after another of the weeds, continually disappointed I assume, and completely ignorant of the cornucopia of petunias in the hanging basket not five feet overhead. Every once in a while she would float up and I would think—there, now she's finally got it! But, so far at least, she has not made the leap. Perhaps it was an aesthetic choice and green is her preference. But the purple and pink treasure remained unclaimed. By the butterfly anyway.

The bee came later. A tiny one—though as scarce as bees have become around here I was glad to see any—found the petunias. But instead of gorging on the large full flowers, he instead insisted on trying to make his way into the nearly closed nearly dead blossoms, skipping entirely the glorious siblings. I watched him disappear into the narrow passage, and could see the from the turbulence outside the tunnel how difficult his passage was. I don't if he made all the way it in, nor what he found when he got there. Maybe he just wanted a challenge. Or maybe the ripened juice is sweeter. Perhaps the bee knew his business better than I.

There are many morals that could be drawn here. But I will leave it to you, and the butterfly, and the bee. My wish is simply this:

May you be fascinated by flowers.

The Spider

A single strand of spider's web was strung across my porch this morning. I would never have seen it if the sun hadn't caught it just right. How in the world could one tiny spider have strung that slender thread, eight feet or more over open space?

Was he saying See what I can do and you can't?

Or was he saying See what can be done?

The truth is, he wasn't saying anything, has no knowledge of me, was just living his life in the world. It's not all about me. I keep forgetting that.

But see what can be done.

I keep forgetting that too.

The Butterfly on the Blossom

We had a guest today.

A butterfly stopped by the azalea outside my window. I was able to get a quick photo. Then he was gone.

After he left, it occurred to me that I didn't feel regret that he was gone. I felt grateful that he had stopped by, that I was there at that moment to see that fleeting convergence.

I find it hard sometimes to recognize the small gifts. But I'm getting better at it. I notice the birds singing more often these days. I'll stop and admire a tree. Or clouds. Or grass. The brilliance of the green in sunlight. Or sunlight, half an hour before sunset when the angle of the light makes everything crystal.

What I have difficulty with, always, is regretting. I don't let things go. People. I don't let people go, even when they have been gone a long time.

Still.

The butterfly is on the blossom.

Rejoice. And be glad.

Thinking Small

When I go for a walk, I often have my head down. So far I haven't bumped into anyone. Or they haven't bumped into me. I suppose social distancing has help, when it comes to that.

I like to think that other sojourners imagine I am deep in thought pondering vast questions of human existence. More likely, they think I am anti-social, which I suppose is partly true.

The real reason I look down as I walk is so I don't step on anyone (or more than one). I am convinced that after death, if there is a tribunal with St. Peter or Rhadamanthus or Anubis, the primary category of judging will be how many beings you have stepped on (or otherwise hurt) and how many saved. And I don't think size matters - a being is a being in my ecosystemic view.

Maybe you even get credit for thinking small.

I believe I am doing well in the Karma department, though I don't have an actual count to offer. Though I'm hoping that beings I can't see don't count, or better that I don't hurt them if I do step on them. There is more biomass in bacteria than in any other form of animal life, so that worries me a bit.

All in all, it makes for a gentle life, seeking goodness where it exists, beauty where it is found, laughter as it comes, and joy in everything. Thinking small makes you a small part of a larger life, instead of a large part of a smaller one. It's worth the tradeoff.

Chapter Two

On Rolls the Old World

One Moment

One moment of serene and confident life is more glorious than a whole campaign of daring:

Henry David Thoreau

Journal, December 1839

Amid the Ruins

We cannot part with our friends. We cannot let our angels go. We do not see that they only go out, that archangels may come in. We are idolaters of the old. We do not believe in the riches of the soul, in its proper eternity and omnipresence. We do not believe there is any force in to-day to rival or recreate that beautiful yesterday. We linger in the ruins of the old tent, where once we had bread and shelter and organs, nor believe that the spirit can feed, cover, and nerve us again. We cannot again find aught so dear, so sweet, so graceful. But we sit and weep in vain. The voice of the Almighty saith, 'Up and onward for evermore!' We cannot stay amid the ruins.

Ralph Waldo Emerson

Compensation

Friendship

I do not wish to treat friendships daintily, but with roughest courage. When they are real, they are not glass threads or frostwork, but the solidest thing we know.

Ralph Waldo Emerson

Friendship

Good to Know

Speak what you think now in hard words, and to-morrow speak what to-morrow thinks in hard words again, though it contradict every thing you said to-day.

Ralph Waldo Emerson

Self-Reliance

Noise

And a little dog, nameless and mongrel and many-fathered, grown, yet weighing less than six pounds, saying as if to itself, I can't be dangerous, because there's nothing much smaller than I am; I can't be fierce, because they would call it just a noise; I can't be humble, because I'm already too close to the ground to genuflect; I can't be proud, because I wouldn't be near enough to it for anyone to know who was casting the shadow, and I don't even know that I'm not going to heaven, because they have already decided that I don't possess an immortal soul. So all I can be is brave. But it's all right. I can be that, even if they still call it just noise.

William Faulkner

The Bear

For Better, For Worse

There is a time in every man's education when he arrives at the conviction that envy is ignorance; that imitation is suicide; that he must take himself for better, for worse, as his portion; that though the wide universe is full of good, no kernel of nourishing corn can come to him but through his toil bestowed on that plot of ground which is given to him to till. The power which resides in him is new in nature, and none but he knows what that is which he can do, nor does he know until he has tried.

Ralph Waldo Emerson

Self-Reliance

In Deed

Where is the love, beauty, and truth we seek But in our mind? and if we were not weak Should we be less in deed than in desire?

Shelley

Julian and Maddalo

Fill the Day

If we filled the day with bravery, we should not shrink from celebrating it.

Ralph Waldo Emerson

The Poet

The New Teacher

I look for the new Teacher, that shall follow so far those shining laws, that he shall see them come full circle; shall see their rounding complete grace; shall see the world to be the mirror of the soul; shall see the identity of the law of gravitation with purity of heart; and shall show that the Ought, that Duty, is one thing with Science, with Beauty, and with Joy.

Ralph Waldo Emerson

Divinity School Address

Dream-Power

Doubt not, O poet, but persist. Say, 'It is in me, and shall out.' Stand there, baulked and dumb, stuttering and stammering, hissed and hooted, stand and strive, until, at last, rage draw out of thee that *dream*-power which every night shows thee is thine own; a power transcending all limit and privacy, and by virtue of which a man is the conductor of the whole river of electricity. Nothing walks, or creeps, or grows, or exists, which must not in turn arise and walk before him as exponent of his meaning. Comes he to that power, his genius is no longer exhaustible.

Ralph Waldo Emerson

The Poet

The Problem

The problem is not so much to see what nobody has yet seen, as to think what nobody has yet thought concerning that which everybody sees.

Arthur Shopenhauer

Parerga und Paralipomena

M. A.

If you work at that which is before you, following right reason seriously, vigorously, calmly, without allowing anything else to distract you, but keeping your divine part pure, as if you might be bound to give it back immediately; if you hold to this, expecting nothing, fearing nothing, but satisfied with your present activity according to nature...you will be happy. And there is no man who is able to prevent this.

Marcus Aurelius

Meditations

Or Mary Alice

The One True Home

Every man, every woman, carries in heart and mind the image of the ideal place, the right place, the one true home, known or unknown, actual or visionary.

Edward Abbey

Desert Solitaire

The Facts Most Astounding

If the day and the night are such that you greet them with joy, and life emits a fragrance like flowers and sweet-scented herbs, is more elastic, more starry, more immortal — that is your success. All nature is your congratulation, and you have cause momentarily to bless yourself. The greatest gains and values are farthest from being appreciated. We easily come to doubt if they exist. We soon forget them. They are the highest reality. Perhaps the facts most astounding and most real are never communicated by man to man. The true harvest of my daily life is somewhat as intangible and indescribable as the tints of morning or evening. It is a little star-dust caught, a segment of the rainbow which I have clutched.

Henry David Thoreau

Walden

The Best Thing for Being Sad

"The best thing for being sad," replied Merlin, beginning to puff and blow, "is to learn something. That's the only thing that never fails. You may grow old and trembling in your anatomies, you may lie awake at night listening to the disorder of your veins, you may miss your only love, you may see the world about you devastated by evil lunatics, or know your honour trampled in the sewers of baser minds. There is only one thing for it then — to learn. Learn why the world wags and what wags it. That is the only thing which the mind can never exhaust, never alienate, never be tortured by, never fear or distrust, and never dream of regretting. Learning is the only thing for you. Look what a lot of things there are to learn."

T.H. White

The Once and Future King

The Question of the Times

To me, however, the question of the times resolved itself into a practical question of the conduct of life. How shall I live? We are incompetent to solve the times. Our geometry cannot span the huge orbits of the prevailing ideas, behold their return, and reconcile their opposition. We can only obey our own polarity.

Ralph Waldo Emerson

The Conduct of Life

That is Morning

To cease for a bright hour to be prisoner of this sickly body and become as large as the World.

Ralph Waldo Emerson

Journal, 1838

The Lessons of Gurnemanz

'And thus I begin, do thou hearken—From true shame shalt thou never flee,

A shameless man, bethink thee, what place in the world hath he?

As a bird that moulteth ever so his honour doth fall away,

And hereafter he hath his portion in the fires of Hell for aye.'

'So noble methinks thy bearing, a folk's Lord thou well mayst be;

If high be thy birth, and yet higher the lot that awaiteth thee,

Then see that thy heart hath pity for the poor and needy man

And fight thou against his sorrow with free gifts as best thou can,

For a true knight must aye be humble—A brave man who need doth know

Full often with shame he battles, and sore is that strife I trow,

For him shall thy help be ready—(Who lighteneth his brother's need

From Heaven he winneth favour as rewarding for righteous deed.)

For in sooth his case is harder than theirs who as beggars stand'

Neath the window, and succour seeking, for bread shall stretch forth the hand.

Thou shalt learn in a fitting measure both rich and poor to be,

Who spendeth as lord at all times no lordly soul hath he—

Yet who heapeth o'er-much his treasure he winneth methinks but shame,

But give thou unto each their honour, so best shalt thou guard thy fame.'

I saw well as thou earnest hither that thou hadst of my counsel need—

Yield not unto ways discourteous but give to thy bearing heed,

Nor be thou so swift to question—Yet I would not that thou withhold

An answer good and fitting to the speech one with thee would hold.

Thou canst hear and see, I wot well full five shalt thy senses be,

An thou use them aright, then wisdom it draweth anear to thee.

'In thy wrath remember mercy, and slay not a conquered foe,

He who to thine arms shall yield him take his pledge and let him go;

Unless he such ill have wrought thee as sorrow of heart doth give,

An my counsel thou fain wouldst follow, then in sooth shalt thou let him live.'

'Full oft shalt thou bear thy harness—When thy knightly task is sped

Thy hands and face thou shalt cleanse them from the rust and the iron red,

For such is in truth thy duty, so thy face shall be fair and bright,

And when maiden's eyes behold thee they shall deem thee a goodly sight.

Be manly and of good courage, so shalt thou deserve thy fame;

Hold women in love and honour, it shall be to thine own good name;

And be ever steadfast-minded as befitteth good man and true,

An with lies thou wouldst fain deceive them much harm can thy dealings do.

If true love be repaid with falsehood then swift shalt the judgment be,

And a speedy end to all honour and renown shall it bring to thee.

As beneath the stealthy footsteps of the thief the dry stick breaks,

And the slumbering watcher, startled, to his danger swiftly wakes

So false ways and dealings crooked in their wake bring but strife and woe;

Prove this by true love, for true women have skill 'gainst the hidden foe,

And their wiles can outweigh his cunning—
An thou winnest from women hate,

Then for ever art thou dishonoured, and shame on thy life shall wait.'

'So take thou to heart my counsel—And more would I tell to thee;

Husband and wife united as one shall they ever be,

As the sun that this morning shineth, and this morn that we call to-day,

So the twain may be sundered never but *one* shall be held alway.

As twin blossoms from one root springing e'en so shall they bloom and grow;

With wisdom receive my counsel that its truth thou hereafter know.'

Wolfram von Eschenbach

Parzifal

Translated by Jessie L. Weston

A Hidden Life

For the growing good of the world is partly dependent on unhistoric acts; and that things are not so ill with you and me as they might have been, is half owing to the number who lived faithfully a hidden life, and rest in unvisited tombs.

George Eliot

Middlemarch

Seasons of the Soul

Who looks in the sun will see no light else; but also he will see no shadow. Our life revolves unceasingly, but the centre is ever the same, and the wise will regard only the seasons of the soul.

Henry David Thoreau

Journal, March 10, 1841

Castles in the Air

If you have built castles in the air, your work need not be lost; that is where they should be. Now put the foundations under them

Henry David Thoreau

Walden

Fishing in the Sky

Time is but the stream I go a-fishing in. I drink at it; but while I drink I see the sandy bottom and detect how shallow it is. Its thin current slides away, but eternity remains. I would drink deeper; fish in the sky, whose bottom is pebbly with stars. I cannot count one. I know not the first letter of the alphabet. I have always been regretting that I was not as wise as the day I was born. The intellect is a cleaver; it discerns and rifts its way into the secret of things. I do not wish to be any more busy with my hands than is necessary. My head is hands and feet. I feel all my best faculties concentrated in it. My instinct tells me that my head is an organ for burrowing, as some creatures use their snout and fore-paws, and with it I would mine and burrow my way through these hills. I think that the richest vein is somewhere hereabouts; so by the divining-rod and thin rising vapors I judge; and here I will begin to mine.

Henry David Thoreau

Walden

Miracles

To me, every hour of the light and dark is a miracle,

Every inch of space is a miracle,

Every square yard of the surface of the earth is spread with the same,

Walt Whitman

Miracles

The Task of the Human-Hearted

The task of the human-hearted man is to procure benefits for the world and to eliminate its calamities. Now among all the current calamities of the world, which are the greatest? I say that attacks on small states by large ones, disturbances of small houses by large ones, oppression of the weak by the strong, misuse of the few by the many, deception of the simple by the cunning, and disdain toward the humble by the honored: these are the mis-fortunes of the world....When we come to think about the causes of all these calamities, how have they arisen? Have they arisen out of love of others and benefiting others? We must reply that it is not so. Rather we should say that they have arisen out of hate of others and injuring others. If we classify those in the world who hate others and injure others, shall we call them 'discriminating' 'all-embracing'? We must say that they are 'discriminating.' So, then, is not mutual discrimination the cause of the major calamities of the world? Therefore the principle of discrimination is wrong.

Mo Tzu

The Mozi

I am Silent

illa cantat; nos tacemus; quando ver venit meum?

(She sings; I am silent; when will my springtime come)

Unknown

The Vigil of Venus

Ephemera

Ah, do not mourn, he said,

That we are tired, for other loves await us

Hate on and love through unrepining hours.

Before us lies eternity; our souls

Are love, and a continual farewell.

W. B Yeats

Ephemera

Unwritten

Ah you still ask me for that unwritten letter always due, it seems, always unwritten, from year to year, by me to you, dear Lidian, -- I fear too more widely than you mean, -- always due & unwritten by me to every sister & brother of the human race. I have only to say that I also bemoan myself daily for the same cause – that I cannot write this letter, that I have not stamina & constitution enough to mind the two functions of seraph and cherub, oh no, let me not use such great words, -- rather say that a photometer cannot be a stove. It must content you for the time, that I truly acknowledge a poverty of nature, & have really no proud defence at all to set up, but ill-health, puniness, and Stygian limitation. Is not the wife too always the complement of the man's imperfections, and mainly of those half men the clerks? Besides am I not , O best Lidian, a most foolish affectionate goodman & papa, with a weak side toward apples & sugar and all domesticities, when I am once in Concord? Answer me that. Well I will come again shortly and behave the best I can Only I foresee plainly that the trick of solitariness never can leave me.

Ralph Waldo Emerson

In a Letter to his wife Lidian

Distance

Visible distance behind and before us, is respectively out image of memory and hope.

Ralph Waldo Emerson

Nature

The Use of Memory

This is the use of memory:

For liberation - not less of love but expanding

Of love beyond desire.

T. S. Eliot
Little Gidding

Natural Literature

And this, our life, exempt from public haunt, finds tongues in trees, books in the running brooks, sermons in stones, and good in everything.

Shakespeare

As You Like It

Living Poetry

There is nothing inorganic... The earth is not a mere fragment of dead history, stratum upon stratum like the leaves of a book, to be studied by geologists and antiquaries chiefly, but living poetry like the leaves of a tree, which precede flowers and fruit -- not a fossil earth, but a living earth

Henry David Thoreau

Walden

Nothing

Nothing can bring you peace but yourself. Nothing can bring you peace but the triumph of principles.

Ralph Waldo Emerson

Self-Reliance

The Danger of Poetry

He repeated, with such tremulous feeling, the various lines which imaged a broken heart, or a mind destroyed by wretchedness, and looked so entirely as if he meant to be understood, that she ventured to hope he did not always read only poetry, and to say, that she thought it was the misfortune of poetry to be seldom safely enjoyed by those who enjoyed it completely; and that the strong feelings which alone could estimate it truly were the very feelings which ought to taste it but sparingly.

Jane Austen

Persuasion

On Rolls the Old World

The two parties which divide the state, the party of Conservatism and that of Innovation, are very old, and have disputed the possession of the world ever since it was made. This quarrel is the subject of civil history. The conservative party established the reverend hierarchies and monarchies of the most ancient world. The battle of patrician and plebeian, of parent state and colony, of old usage and accommodation to new facts, of the rich and the poor, reappears in all countries and times. The war rages not only in battle-fields, in national councils, and ecclesiastical synods, but agitates every man's bosom with opposing advantages every hour. On rolls the old world meantime, and now one, now the other gets the day, and still the fight renews itself as if for the first time, under new names and hot personalities.

STEPHEN EVANS

Ralph Waldo Emerson

The Conservative

Little

United there is little we cannot do in a host of cooperative ventures. Divided there is little we can do -- for we dare not meet a powerful challenge at odds and split asunder.

John F. Kennedy

Inaugural Address

Or

Men are born for each other. So either teach or tolerate.

Marcus Aurelius

Meditations

Democracy, You Say

I enjoy democracy immensely. It is incomparably idiotic, and hence incomparably amusing. Does it exalt dunderheads, cowards, trimmers, frauds, cads? Then the pain of seeing them go up is balanced and obliterated by the joy of seeing them come down. Is it inordinately wasteful, extravagant, dishonest? Then so is every other form of government: all alike are enemies to laborious and virtuous men. Is rascality at the very heart of it? Well, we have borne that rascality since 1776, and continue to survive. In the long run, it may turn out that rascality is necessary to human government, and even to civilization itself - that civilization, at bottom, is nothing but a colossal swindle. I do not know: I report only that when the suckers are running well the spectacle is infinitely exhilarating. But I am, it may be, a somewhat malicious man: my sympathies, when it comes to suckers, tend to be coy. What I can't make out is how any man can believe in democracy who feels for and with them, and is pained when they are debauched and made a show of. How can any man be a democrat who is sincerely a democrat?

H. L. Menken

Last Words

The Powerful Play

The question, O me! so sad, recurring—
What good amid these, O me, O life?

Answer.

That you are here—that life exists, and identity;

That the powerful play goes on, and you will contribute a verse.

Walt Whitman

O Me! O Life!

I Would Translate If I Could

el suo profondo vidi che s'interna,

legato con amore in un volume,

ciò che per l'universo si squaderna

Dante

Paradiso

Certainty

As far as the laws of mathematics refer to reality, they are not certain; and as far as they are certain, they do not refer to reality.

Albert Einstein

Address to the Prussian Academy of Sciences

Success

If the day and the night are such that you greet them with joy, and life emits a fragrance like flowers and sweet-scented herbs, is more elastic, more starry, more immortal — that is your success. All nature is your congratulation, and you have cause momentarily to bless yourself. The greatest gains and values are farthest from being appreciated. We easily come to doubt if they exist. We soon forget them. They are the highest reality. Perhaps the facts most astounding and most real are never communicated by man to man. The true harvest of my daily life is somewhat as intangible and indescribable as the tints of morning or evening. It is a little star-dust caught, a segment of the rainbow which I have clutched.

Henry David Thoreau

Walden

In Common Hours

If one advances confidently in the direction of his dreams, and endeavors to live the life which he has imagined, he will meet with a success unexpected in common hours.

Henry David Thoreau

Walden

One Direction

Each man has his own vocation. The talent is the call. There is one direction in which all space is open to him. He has faculties silently inviting him thither to endless exertion. He is like a ship in a river; he runs against obstructions on every side but one; on that side all obstruction is taken away, and he sweeps serenely over a deepening channel into an infinite sea. This talent and this call depend on his organization, or the mode in which the general soul incarnates itself in him. He inclines to do something which is easy to him, and good when it is done, but which no other man can do. He has no rival.

Ralph Waldo Emerson

Spiritual Laws

Of Truth

What is truth? said jesting Pilate, and would not stay for an answer. Certainly there be, that delight in giddiness, and count it a bondage to fix a belief; affecting free-will in thinking, as well as in acting. And though the sects of philosophers of that kind be gone, yet there remain certain discoursing wits, which are of the same veins, though there be not so much blood in them, as was in those of the ancients. But it is not only the difficulty and labor, which men take in finding out of truth, nor again, that when it is found, it imposeth upon men's thoughts, that doth bring lies in favor; but a natural though corrupt love, of the lie itself. One of the later school of the Grecians, examineth the matter, and is at a stand, to think what should be in it, that men should love lies; where neither they make for pleasure, as with poets, nor for advantage, as with the merchant; but for the lie's sake. But I cannot tell; this same truth, is a naked, and open day-light, that doth not show the masks, and mummeries, and triumphs, of the world, half so stately and daintily as candle-lights. Truth may perhaps come to the price of a pearl, that showeth best by day; but it will not rise to the price of a diamond, or carbuncle, that showeth best in varied lights. A mixture of a lie doth ever add pleasure. Doth any man doubt, that if there were taken out of men's minds, vain opinions, flattering hopes, false valuations, imaginations as one would, and the like, but it would leave the minds, of a number of men, poor shrunken things, full of melancholy and indisposition, and unpleasing to themselves?

Francis Bacon

Essayes or Counsels, Civill and Morall, 1625

The Secret of Culture

The secret of culture is to learn, that a few great points steadily reappear, alike in the poverty of the obscurest farm, and in the miscellany of metropolitan life, and that these few are alone to be regarded, — the escape from all false ties; courage to be what we are; and love of what is simple and beautiful; independence, and cheerful relation, these are the essentials, — these, and the wish to serve, — to add somewhat to the well-being of men.

Ralph Waldo Emerson

Culture

The Coming of Dusk

At times I believe that my feet have been set upon a road which I shall go on following, and that slowly the centre of gravity of my being will shift over from the world of day, from the domain of organizing and regulating universal powers, into the world of Imagination. Already now I feel, as when at the age of twenty I was going to a ball in the evening, that day is a space of time without meaning, and that it is with the coming of dusk, with the lighting of the first star and the first candle, that things will become what they really are, and will come forth to meet me.

Karen Blixen (Isak Dinesen)

Shadows in the Grass

Unsettling

Do not set the least value on what I do, or the least discredit on what I do not, as if I pretended to settle any thing as true or false. I unsettle all things.

Ralph Waldo Emerson

Circles

A Palpable Movement

To persons standing alone on a hill during a clear mid-night such as this, the roll of the world eastward is almost a palpable movement. The sensation may be caused by the panoramic glide of the stars past earthly objects, which is perceptible in a few minutes of stillness, or by a fancy that the better outlook upon space afforded by a hill emphasizes terrestrial revolution, or by the wind, or by the solitude; but whatever be its origin, the impression of riding along is vivid and abiding. The poetry of motion is a phrase much in use, and to enjoy the epic form of that gratification it is necessary to stand on a hill at a small hour of the night, and, first enlarging the consciousness with a sense of difference from the mass of civilized mankind, who are horizontal and disregardful of all such proceedings at this time, long and quietly watch your stately progress through the stars. After such a nocturnal reconnoitre among these astral clusters, aloft from the customary haunts of thought and vision, some men may feel raised to a capability for eternity at once.

Thomas Hardy

Far from the Madding Crowd

Respect

the delicate ecology of your delusions.

Tony Kushner

Angels in America

The Other Side of Silence

If we had a keen vision and feeling of all ordinary human life, it would be like hearing the grass grow and the squirrel's heart beat, and we should die of that roar which lies on the other side of silence.

George Eliot

Middlemarch

Walking Home

To finish the moment, to find the journey's end in every step of the road, to live the greatest number of good hours, is wisdom.

Ralph Waldo Emerson

Experience

I Wonder

Let others wrangle. I will wonder.

St. Augustine

Courtesy Ralph Waldo Emerson

Joy

Even where there is no happiness, there is the next joy and the next.

The trick is to look.

Me

CHAPTER THREE

Heard in a Dream

Don't

put on sunglasses before you leave the house. There is too much too beautiful to see.

Whence and Whither

The whence of beauty always is unclear. The whither, that we know, is far from here.

The Summoning of Courage

is the most dangerous of spells. For you cannot summon courage to do one thing. You must summon courage to do all things.

Reach for the Moon

If you miss, you end up in the cold dead vacuum of space. But it's beautiful out there and the moon's not much better really.

Heard in a Dream

Do not open the silence. Let the silence open you.

Gratitude

Being grateful for the life you never planned takes planning.

Spin

Don't we all?

As a Rule

Rule of Life 1: do the most you can for the most you can.

Rule of Life 2: Include yourself in Rule 1.

The First Truth of Life

You are going to die. It may be that the soul will live on after you die. You are not the soul. You are a conscious living entity. You are going to die.

Some Mistakes

You make anyway.

Destiny

is making the right mistake.

Golf Wisdom

You always make the last putt.

Taut

The lesson is the lesson.

Go Figure

It is the steps that make the path.

Once Before I Go

I need to tell you.

1,2,...

When I try to make every minute count, I end up just counting the minutes.

People

care about different things the same and the same things differently.

Maybe

there would be more grace in the world if there were more grace in the world.

Divine

When God closes a door, he opens a window. Then he throws you out of it.

The Key to Life

is you don't need a key. It was never locked.

Nothing

When nothing can be done, nothing is everything.

Kindness

An act of kindness is like a stone thrown into a great lake. The tiny waves move out until they cannot be seen, but always return again, though they may go unnoticed in stormy waters.

Sadness

is like the ring of a tree. We grow around it but it is always there. And in the winter that growth is slow.

Grief

is a response, not a process. You are the process.

Consciousness

is the thin veneer covering the engine of instinct.

Ontology

I know what I am. Learning what I am not is a continual education.

The Key Drawer

I measure my life in mystery keys, that open locks forgotten now or lost.

What Dreams May Not Come

I have been thinking today not about my dreams, but about what I used to dream and don't anymore. I suspect at my age what is missing is as telling as what is there.

In the Time It Takes You

Time takes you.

Is This Happiness?

What's missing in my life has been missing so long I don't miss it anymore.

The Morning After Rain

the stream remembers.

Is There Memory in Eternity?

Or eternity in memory?

Come Again

It takes time to create eternity.

Everything Lasts Forever

Just not all at once.

The Expanding Universe Explained

It's not that the universe is expanding. It's that everything is shrinking, as we are siphoned off into Eternity.

It's Time

for the Timeless.

Sometimes

only poetry is possible.

Just Say Yes

If God gave us a mind to understand, to believe or disbelieve is to reject the gift.

Truth

It is not foolish to pursue truth in the absence of a language capable of expressing it. But it's no picnic.

Truth Again

When you're reaching for the truth, be sure your hand is open. Otherwise, you're punching the truth.

Truth Again

Always tell the kindest truth.

Truth Again

The truth is unwritten, but not unwritable.

Maybe

there would be more grace in the world if there were more grace in the world.

Randomness

seems unlikely.

Quantum Credo

With God, all things are probable.

With a Nod to Anselm

Nothing is more difficult than nothing. Which is why there is something.

Some

do not go gentle into that good night. Some know it is the night that they are leaving.

Patterns

The *Journey of Etana*. Dante's *Commedia*. The ancient patterns of our spiritual longing evolve but never resolve.

I Wish

I could take a picture of what I see when my eyes are closed.

A World Apart

The thing about living on a sphere is that as you are drifting apart you are also coming together.

The Trick

Imagine now as you will remember then.

Directions

All roads lead to whoever builds the roads.

Which Way

Is the snowflake facing?

Index by Title

Acknowledgements

Many of these pieces have appeared on The Green Room at:

https://www.gr8word.com

About the Author

Stephen Evans is a playwright and the author of *The Island of Always, Painting Sunsets, A Transcendental Journey, Funny Thing Is: A Guide to understanding Comedy; Painting Sunsets*, and other books. Find him online at:

https://www.istephenevans.com/

https://www.facebook.com/iStephenEvans

https://twitter.com/iStephenEvans

CPSIA information can be obtained
at www.ICGtesting.com
Printed in the USA
LVHW031520261121
704539LV00006B/451

9 781953 725165